PLOP!

BY MARTIN BAXENDALE

Published by Silent But Deadly Publications,
21 Bisley Road, Stroud, Glos. GL5 1HF

ISBN 0 9513542 0 5

Printed in Britain by Stoate & Bishop Printers Ltd, Cheltenham, Glos

PLOP!
DRRRiNG! DRRRiNG!
CLicK!
Hello?
No, I'm Sorry...
he's just
plopped out

Judging by the Skid-marks, he must have been doing at least eighty!

TURDO
THE MAGICIAN
VANISHING CABINET
TAP! TAP!
VANISHING CABINET
VANISHING CABINET
SWOOSH!
GURGLE!

MATERNITY WARD
No thanks... we want the birth to be as **natural** as possible

....Plop-plops...Pooh-poohs...Big-jobs....
NAME YOUR BABY

You will meet a long dark stranger

Tra-la-la...
SCRUB
SPLOSH

Sod it...
no paper!
DRIP
DRIP
DRIP

SPLASH
Dust to dust... splashes to splashes...
SWOOSH

GURGLE

SWOOSH
SWOOSH

SWOOSH
SWOOSH
SWOOSH
SWOOSH

SOLARIUM
SUN BED
SUN BED

I must go down to the sea again,
the lonely sea and the sky....
POEMS
POETRY
READING

Don't you dare tramp those muddy boots across my clean floor
SPLUDGE
SPLUDGE
SPLUDGE

CHARITY DIARRHOEA
FUN-RUNS
BANG
SPLURRP!
SPLURRP!
SPLURRP!
SPLURRP!
SPLURRP!
SPLURRP!

Heard the one about the diarrhoea....
CAR WASH
...who lost his job because of sloppy workmanship!
SWOOSH
SPLOSH

Worst case of **peanuts** I've ever seen.....

SPLOSH
SPLOSH

?
SPLUDGE
SPLOSH
SPLOSH

SUICIDE
NOTE

SNIFF
SNIFF
Phew!

PSSSSST!
UNDER-
ARM

Lovely day for a trip to the seaside
SEWAGE

I am **not** a **number** !
No. 2
APOLOGIES TO THE CREATORS OF 'THE PRISONER' SERIES

THE TURDS
SCREAM!
SCREAM!
CLONK!
Read all abaht it....Shit hits fan....
DAILY TURD
DAILY TURD
RIOT AT PLOP CONCERT

No, we didn't plan it... he was an **accident**
GOO-GOO!
RATTLE!

It's amazing how quickly this **bum-music** recording gets him off to sleep
BABY SOOTHER TAPE
SNORE SNORE
PLOP
PLOP
FART
GLOOP
PLOP
GURGLE
FART
PLOP
PLOP
PLOP

FARP!

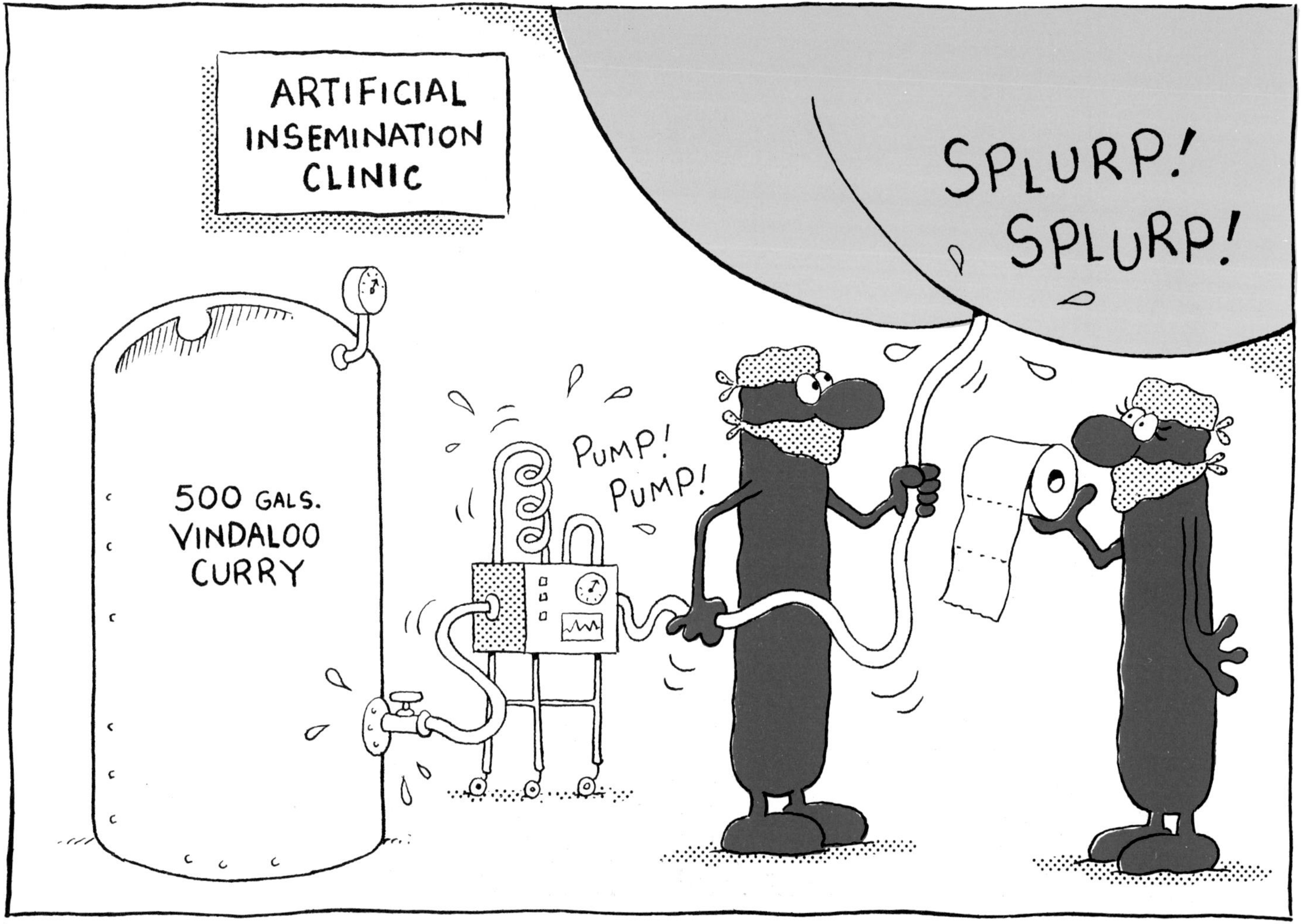
ARTIFICIAL INSEMINATION CLINIC
SPLURP! SPLURP!
500 GALS. VINDALOO CURRY
PUMP! PUMP!

No, of course I don't believe in ghosts...
PHARP!

Surf's up!
FLUSH!
SWOOSH!

I'm faeces... what's your star sign?

THE END
Dunno about you... but I thought that was a load of crap!